For Elijah ...

LOVE LIFE

Micheal O'Siadhail

St. Andrews

16 XI 2009

Micheal O'Siadhail was born in 1947. He was educated at Clongowes Wood College, Trinity College Dublin, and the University of Oslo. A full-time writer, he has published eleven collections of poetry. He was awarded an Irish American Cultural Institute prize for poetry in 1982, and the Marten Toonder Prize for Literature in 1998. His poem suites, *The Naked Flame*, *Summerfest*, *Crosslight* and *Dublin Spring* were commissioned and set to music for performance and broadcasting.

His latest collections are *Our Double Time* (1998), *The Gossamer Wall: poems in witness to the Holocaust* (2002) and *Love Life* (2005), all published by Bloodaxe. *Hail! Madam Jazz: New and Selected Poems* (Bloodaxe Books, 1992) included selections from six of his collections, *The Leap Year* (1978), *Rungs of Time* (1980), *Belonging* (1982), *Springnight* (1983), *The Image Wheel* (1985), as well as the whole of *The Chosen Garden* (1990) and a new collection *The Middle Voice* (1992). A new selection of his earlier poetry, *Poems 1975-1995*, drawing on both *Hail! Madam Jazz* and his later collection *A Fragile City* (Bloodaxe Books, 1995), was published by Bloodaxe in 1999.

He has given poetry readings and broadcast extensively in Ireland, Britain, Europe, North America and Japan. In 1985 he was invited to give the Vernam Hull Lecture at Harvard and the Trumbull Lecture at Yale University. He represented Ireland at the Poetry Society's European Poetry Festival in London in 1981. He was writer-in-residence at the Yeats Summer School in 1991 and at the Frankfurt Bookfair in 1997.

He has been a lecturer at Trinity College Dublin and a professor at the Dublin Institute for Advanced Studies. Among his many academic works are *Learning Irish* (Yale University Press, 1988) and *Modern Irish* (Cambridge University Press, 1989). He was a member of the Arts Council of the Republic of Ireland (1988-93) and of the Advisory Committee on Cultural Relations (1989-97), a founder member of Aosdána (Academy of distinguished Irish artists) and a former editor of *Poetry Ireland Review*. He is the founding chairman of ILE (Ireland Literature Exchange), and was a judge for *The Irish Times* ESB 1998 Theatre Awards and the 1998 *Sunday Tribune*/Hennessy Cognac Literary Awards.

Micheal O'Siadhail's website: www.osiadhail.com

MICHEAL O'SIADHAIL

Love Life

BLOODAXE BOOKS

First published 2005 by
Bloodaxe Books Ltd,
Highgreen,
Tarset,
Northumberland NE48 1RP.

www.bloodaxebooks.com
For further information about Bloodaxe titles
please visit our website or write to
the above address for a catalogue.

Bloodaxe Books Ltd acknowledges
the financial assistance of
Arts Council England, North East.

Cover printing by J. Thomson Colour Printers Ltd, Glasgow.

Printed in Great Britain by
Bell & Bain Limited, Glasgow, Scotland.

For Bríd

Three dozen years. Morning, noon, night.
Love life. Our being bathèd in the light.

ACKNOWLEDGEMENTS

Acknowledgements are due to the editors of the following publications in which some of these poems first appeared: *Carolina Quarterly*, *The Clifton Anthology* (Clifton Community Arts Week, 2002), *David Jones Society Journal*, *Goethe: Musical Poet, Musical Catalyst* (Carysfort Press 2004), *New Hibernian Review*, *Orbis*, *Other Poetry*, *Stories for Jamie* (Blackwater Press, 2002), *The Times Literary Supplement*, *Triquarterly*, and *The Way You Say the World:a celebration for Anne Stevenson* (Shoestring Press, 2003); and to RTÉ Radio where a number of these poems were broadcast.

CONTENTS

CRIMSON THREAD

Your lips are like a crimson thread
and your mouth is lovely…

Song of Solomon

Homing

1

Longbow years of longing
Bends an arc's wooden U.
Tenser stretch, fiercer shoot.

An arrow rigs a violent route
Gathering into a shaft of yew
Dreamed eye of a golden ring.

Cupidinous. Desire overdue
A goose cock-feather quivering.
No hard-to-get. No pursuit.

Come what may. *Coûte que coûte.*
I finger a silk whipped string.
My life takes aim for you.

2

O Eros ravish and enlarge us.
Just to gaze, to listen, to mingle.
Sweet fusion. Carnal relish.
Break me again with outlandish
Desire my prowling Mademoiselle.
The arrow of our time discharges.

3

A shaft so full of amorous remembering,
Déjà vu of yearning's consummate fit
As I stoop to fondle a hollow in your nape.

As if such hunger coiled up in a man
Wakes some reminiscence we relearn
I kiss in your flesh your spirit's kiss

Like Hermes' son fallen for Salmacis.
Our nature divides only to return.
I've known you since the world began.

A woman's desire now bends to shape
The long elucidation of my spirit.
An arrow homes into its golden ring.

Long Song

Fragrance of your oils.
L'amour fou. Such sweet folly.
Your haunting presence
Distilled traces of perfume.
Resonances of voice
Dwell in my nervous body.
My skin wants to glow,
All of my being glistens.
Divine shining through.
Your lips like a crimson thread,
Your mouth is lovely...
You're all beautiful, my love.
Honeyed obsession
Of unreasonable love.
Pleased, being pleased,
I caress this amplitude,
Eternal roundness.
Voluptuous golden ring.
Sap and juices sing
Eden's long song in the veins.
Spirit into flesh.
The flesh into the spirit.
A garden fountain,
A well of living water,
Flowing streams from Lebanon.

For Real

A first gazing at you unawares.
Wonder by wonder my body savours

The conch-like detail of an ear,
An amethyst ring on your finger.

Could I ever have enough of you?
Juiced cantaloupe, ripe honeydew,

Slack desire so I desire you more.
Laugh as no one laughed before.

Vivid more vivid, real more real.
I stare towards heavens you reveal.

Yellower yellow. Bluer blue.
Can you see me as I see you?

Sweeter than being loved to love.
Sweetest our beings' hand in glove.

Milk and honey, spice and wine.
I'm your lover. You are mine.

Candle

I think I've fallen in love again with Eve
Who coded your genes so perfectly for me
And sent them replicating down an aeon.

With every needed break or loss or siege
Chromosomes mutate to bring you in the nick
Of time to be this beloved face and name.

Amazed once more I hardly dare to believe
I fall heir to whatever you choose in me;
Fluke and mould of planned unplanned liaison.

Shulammite, Laura, Beatrice, Bríd.
In double corded spirals of a candle's wick
After such ages helixes of yearning flame.

Healing

Think that I might never have happened on you,
Mate and match;
For all the work of genes so many *ifs*.

Supposing in the bebop and noise of youth,
In turns and riffs,
In fumbled serendipities of time and place

I'd faltered or somehow failed to recognise
My counter-face
Or Eros hadn't led across the Rubicon?

Imagine we weren't ripe for one another –
Me blundering on,
Strung up, burning the candle at both ends –

Or if I hadn't suffered breakage under way?
The broken mends.
Burnt not shy. Wounded enough to heal.

Complementarity

Golden halo of early lust,
Arrow that trembles and aches
In a looped bow of suspense

And still delights in anticipation,
Part an aiming and part
A relished moment loth

To let go the silk string.
So, the Rubicon.
Yield and quiver of returning

Until we two are each and both
Wave and fired dart,
A misty integration.

Soft combat. Honeyed violence.
My female being awakes
Dewy-eyed with trust.

Sun

A fireball I cannot hold a candle to –
Light-years more giving, ample and rife
With desire, magnolia chalice of body

I touch petal by petal and undo.
Like an overcoat a wife must last for life
My poor sober father had cautioned me.

Paced madness. Patient furnace of sun.
Shape me, kiln me, cast me, love me,
Mate, mistress, queen, courtesan in one.

Our naked nothing. Wing-giving delirium.
All caution to winds and kings of Jericho,
In Rahab's window tie a crimson thread.

Jag of bliss. Drowsed and overcome
My life for yours. Ravish me! I grow
I sweat, I ripen in your pleasured bed.

Name-dropping

Do friends notice when often by design
I somehow steer the conversation around

So casually to seem to drop your name,
The once-tapped *r* and long *ee* sound,

Charge of a consonant and vowel spliced
Slipping you in like a hidden billet-doux

As though apart I need to stake my claim
On this lovely incantation of your *Geist*?

How even in your absence I conjure you.
I've called you by name. You are mine.

Filling In

Beyond a springboard of concupiscence
All the morning-after tête-à-têtes

Unfold and fill the years of fancy-free;
Optative mood, co-optive present tense

Of past friends we both promise to share,
Stories that we now want to turn to faces.

Early tentative encounters, our début,
Friend by friend, coming out as a pair.

The shock to find so many *you*s in you
And still refind the *you* who chooses me.

Slow transfer and knitting in of kismet.
We move among others who move in us.

Yearning

Though not here Madam
Your body still haunts me
With its scented rockaby.

You go and silence falls
Flake by numbing flake
Across a forlorn room.

Alone and too entire,
Self-contained entropy,
A too perfect balance

Craves again a *jouissance*
To break and shatter me.
I wobble in my desire.

A night's noiseless boom
Of absence and how I wake
As my fumbling hand recalls

Glance and shapes of a thigh.
What yearnings for eternity
Burn in my dreamy palm?

Wobble

Deep down am I already sure of you?
At first green moments, even jealous

Huff and puff of childish self-defence;
Boy sores, gaps and rifts of confidence.

Does a world of eyes see what I too see?
Iago drops a scented handkerchief in me

A night you climb my stairs on tiptoes
To tell how a flame returned to propose.

The dull Moor in me imagines Cassio.
Soft you. A word or two before you go

Promise me our years of trust and ease.
What wound did ever heal but by degrees?

Wound

So and so our wound and mingled yarn,
Lovers' daylight knockabout:
'Who, tell me, said that I said that?'

'Yes, but you're the one who started it!'
Infinite retrospect unfurled
As each other word borrows another tiff.

Was it me snapping at you began the row,
Calling your concern a nag,
All my blustering a hidden self-reproach?

No good the 'Let's call it quits' approach.
I hoist surrender's flag;
My climbing down the only let up now.

Hands in the air. A white handkerchief.
With you I take on the world.
A flaw, maybe, in love I cannot fight.

Eros Venusson smiles at such a spat.
Our making up a making out.
A fabric stitched and toughened in its darn.

Making Up

A male mix of inroad and protection
As I play my part and counterpart,
A pioneer and wooing troubadour

And Madam is my slowing sorcerer
Both holding back and drawing on
As waves of pleasure ebb and flow.

In our marrow drunken angels waft.
See how my soul breathes and glitters,
How I invade and spill my joy in you.

A cry and shiver as *entre nous*
A pebble of desire hops and skitters,
Shimmering in the sea's dark shaft.

Rise and flood, the slack and low
In the moon-pull, the earth-melodeon,
What infinite arousal are we made for?

Ancient *tristesse. La petite mort.*
So must we die? Must we part?
Native of Eden, I ache for resurrection.

Launch

1 *Knot*

Right over left and left over right.
Or the other way around. Symmetrical plot
Of two mutual loops drawn tight,
The squared-off weftage of a reef-knot.

Double and single, a riddle of ligature.
Functional beauty sacred and profane;
A history of knots, a rope architecture,
Easy to loosen but tighter under strain.

Plied strength in our tying up of ends,
An emblem, one tiny glorious detail,
A sign becoming what a sign intends.
We tauten the love-knot, hoist the sail.

2 *Splice*

Braid by braid to unravel
Our weave as stripped
We intersperse
For better, for worse
Our strands; a whipped
And knitted re-ravel

No longer a knot with its come
And go but more
To have and hold
Our splice's twofold
Purchase, a rapport
Tougher than its sum.

I take whoever you are
Or come to be
Till one of us perish
To love, to cherish.
Steer by my burgee.
I hitch to your star.

3 Hitch

A moon hoops earth and earth the sun
Planet hitched to planet, swung like a stone

Hoisted into the taut whirlwind of a sling.
A month's wax and wane, neap and spring,

The tides of things, our orbits loop and pitch.
What is this trust which underwrites a voyage?

Our world-weight and giddy let-fly, a tense
Counterpoise of gravity and centrifugence,

Outward gyres held by their contrary force,
Some push and pull that covenants a universe.

4 Plunge

A balanced helm, a beautiful sail trim.
But over again surge and sweet of deviation ;
A moment's perfect bearing another interim,
Our ark of covenant still steered by variation.
Under a bowl of sky watch and weather-eye
Alert to luff and camber, telltale breath;
Close-hauling, compromise of full and by
And how *the wind bloweth as it listeth*.
That perfect bearing already a moment ago.
Are lovers trimmers? O my Ulysses
Sail on, sail on! Our fleeting *status quo*,
Perfection neared in a series of near misses.
Globed in a bowl of oil, a gimballed compass
Bobs and pivots to hold its northern promise.

Voyage

1 *Reckoning*

After the offing, below an arc of skyline
A passage dips behind a glimpsed horizon,
A mirage that beckons and recedes to where
We think we travel, felt somehow our future
Lay, the position line, our plotted course
That didn't count sudden squalls or detours
We now dead-reckon, things so sure on land
As charts and tidal curves once gone beyond
A harbour arms now so unknown and giddy
And we're in our element and still all at sea.
Pinching hard we narrow down an airflow
To thud the waves to leeward El Dorado;
Ease the sheets a touch then bear away
But re-gathering speed luff up to stay
As near on course as can be as we begin
To fathom a long haul's mode and routine;
Steady notchings on a sheet winch's ratchet
Beyond our first beam reaches of delight.

2 *Log*

Who'll take the tiller? Whose hour? Whose turn?
Rites and habits of each;
Day by day by day a ballast of pattern.

The lovely bulb of a spinnaker blooms on a run;
Then, on a beat our stubborn
Keel counter-drives and harrows us on.

And how many different tacks? Our two lives
Even still at one;
A hull's streamline moments as it connives

With cloth and tide and bearing, glorious reach
Of a vessel that never arrives,
Years logged in schedules of vigil and watch.

3 Echo-sounder

A life's canonical rhythm,
Monk-like tempo of days;
Muscle, sinew, limb
Learn mundane strategies,

Passages crossed, re-crossed,
Courses steered by degrees
As a pianist's fingered trust
Sleeps across the keys

Or wrist movements retain
Ordered strokes of Chinese
Characters, a graven routine
Which both ties and frees.

Hoists and binds that gird
Days of rites and liturgies,
Halyard and curtain cord
Clothes lines, hanked stays.

Echos in a mind's chamber
As a boat heels and sways
Stirs a cradle we remember
To lull a freshening breeze.

A wind-moment's once-off
And ready-about novices
We wear our habits of love.
Even keel of our ease.

Below

The companion way
Down into our boat's hollow.
A whelk's honed spiral.

Cooped and warm below;
Lockers, a galley and bunks.
Children playing house.

This cabin all our homes:
Parnell Street to Booterstown.
A tortoise desire.

Shells we didn't build,
Houses just loaned to live in,
Hermit crabs squatting.

At last Trimleston.
Our pebble-dashed habitat.
Clams exude their shell.

Trimleston

1

Premises hereinafter described and intended
A plot of ground at Trimleston, Booterstown,
Parish of Taney, part Barony of Rathdown
Shown on the map therein outlined in red.
The way we'd only taken just minutes to decide
And yet how it's years before our lives are sewn
Into the fabric of these walls' brick and stone,
Our plot and promise shaped slowly from inside.
Immediately we'd loved the house's light and feel.
Demised unto the said William Henry Watson,
To Cecil William Buggy, to Eileen Dundon...
Our turn to set our hands and affix our seal
In the presence of all who named these rooms home;
Our dreams their memories woven on one loom.

2

But is this house chameleon?
Different modes and shapes
As pictures drawn by a child,
Moods coloured in crayon.

Hail on the window and again
Snug and huddling schoolboy
I nestle in a garden dugout
My secret fort and den.

And when the wind blows
My garret is a tree-house
Slung and roofed in an elm,
Hideaway of reverie that knows

Lone watches before the mast,
The lookout's agony,
Cries of sirens in the marrow.
Rootless me. And you rootfast

Embedded, indigenous, earthbound,
Deepen canals of nutrients,
Limbs' mirror image
Anchoring underground

My crow's nest and hermitage.
Rockaby treetop dreamer
And when the bough breaks?
I feed once more on your rootage.

3

The Whit-weekend we came were we aware
The loom would shuttle here our middle years?
Lovemaking, meals, guests, moments of despair,
For all our secrets here these walls have ears.
To perform and observe covenants contained within
Which expression where context admits or requires
Shall include what is and what might have been
The yin and yang of even our silent desires.
By diverse main assurances and acts in law,
Events and ultimately by indenture of assignment...
Haunts of others' memories bought and sold.
Throughout May we'd talked of plans and paint,
Children with crayons, bricks and straw,
Dream and mortar of promise. Delicate roothold.

Dwelling

1

Our passion's juices coil piecemeal in;
Delights of flesh, oil and ooze of core,
Being hugged in an inner porous skin,
Small beginnings of less becoming more.
Gentle leakings, a gradual *savoir-faire*,
Drip by drip a mantle secretes its lime
As calcium hardens to seal an outer layer
And molluscs secrete their own good time.
A clam distils its house as needs may be;
Always complete and still scales accrue,
Whatever calcareous dreams years filter
From inside out, a slow process of beauty,
Contours and angles of life seeping through;
Our geometry of warmth, shell and shelter.

2

Season by season
Slopes of light that home
Our daily rondo

To caress a horizon,
To fondle how our bedroom
Curtains with Navaho

Designs emblazon
Slants of wall with autumn
So it's as though

It stands to reason
Brick and mortar enwomb
Our being and know

The stairway's treason
Of creaks and humdrum
Whinges, the tiptoe

Of Rilke's frozen
Music in the shell we assume,
Ebb and flow

Of suns that crimson
The sea-urchin's dome
In our gable window.

3

Patterns just understood, thoughts unsaid
House habits, order and rule of our cloister;
Squatter's rights to chairs or sides of a bed,
In rooms of dailyness, the world our oyster.
Do steady minds make everything their own?
In a bivalve's hollow even the tiniest grain
Layered over can work a precious stone,
Love's somnambulance and legerdemain.
The up-and-over door a castle drawbridge,
Our converted attic crow's nest and garret,
Under the drain cover outside the garage
The Count of Monte Cristo's oubliette.
In the clammy ear of a mollusc oceans swell;
Grit that sands and pearls our chosen shell.

Guests

1

Our dugout, lair, our haunt, fort and den.
Snuggle and crouch of a schoolboy hideaway;
First delight of privacies but soon again
A deeper urge to invite others into play.
As a Chinese sign with a treadle hindering a gate,
A single word for both barrier and concern –
The nestling exclusion of our tête-à-tête,
Withdrawal and marking off the better to return.
Cloister and burrow, whispering inner sanctum,
Our bolthole and refuge, our own place apart,
Hugger-mugger of warmth through thick and thin
With doors that close only to disclose a welcome.
Space for munificence. Open hand. Open heart.
Steadiness of seclusion becoming a beckoning in.

2

A thought through menu.
Their last visit what was it?
Enough white and red?
A day preparing *la cuisine*.
Dressed up and ready,
House-proud excitement of hosts
Blue napkins folded
And tall glasses anxious.
To bring extra chairs,
To fix our table placings,
We check kitchen timings,
Guessing the first to arrive.

Boisterous humour,
Conversations tuning up,
An evening's wine
And food weave their dynamic.
Gossip, jokes, flirtings,
Things partners didn't dare say,

Watch

1

Transit of dreams, rite of passage
As a pencil traces ground tracks
Skims and plots
A course, harbours of refuge
Charts, almanacs,
Pilot books, our rate of knots.

First intimacy, the in-your-face
Of loneliness dares now accept
A middle distance,
Delicate growing space
Of watches kept
Across beam and draft of silence.

Mute nearness, sweet abyss,
High and low waters of mood,
Time and tide;
Love weathers to what is,
An ease and latitude,
Parallels that needn't meet.

To know enough to know hiddenness,
Sunken hulks, an unmarked ridge
Or reef or shelf.
To have and never possess;
Each a hermitage,
Cave of heart, cache of self.

Chartered years of bell-shaped lead-lines,
Riptides, overfalls, height and shallow.
So much unfathomed.
A sandbank drifts and realigns.
Echo by echo,
Shoal by shoal an ocean plumbed.

2

A fresh turn of phrase
The flurry and throb
Of words tuned for a first time.

Often with strangers
A surprise role shift,
A different demeanour.

Some detail untold:
'I must have mentioned that?'
Sudden sidelong playful air.

Staunch in narrow straits,
Steady in squalls like
A craft closer to the wind.

Explorer's pleasure
In unworn waters
Another channel charted.

Still sides never shown,
Faces unseen before
Glanced through our darkened glass.

3

Each shape and lineament of day by day,
Positions to plot or check in nightly dialogue,
Line of sounding along our double headway,
Intimacies of thoughts we share and log.
To follow every knot, warm and close-up
And yet to hold the near and far in balance
As if we slacken a little to allow for scope,
Lull and driftage, love's adaptive distance.
Dreamy horizons outline another reality
As finer details cross the mind's screen;
Turn and turn about and still to watch
Moments shifting focus as needs may be,
Zero-in, drawing back or in between;
Chart scale and voyage we make and match.

About

1

Habits and habitat
Everyday this and that
Of nod and half-response
Or crossed communiqué
But what had you started to say?
As if a broken utterance

Like the chatter of the gone
Somehow travels on
Infinite megahertz
Lurks forever in the ether
Of some promised weather
Or in the hum between the words

The boat's radio
Suddenly blurts below
The deck. Channel 16
Hisses and waits to snatch
Alerts or warn; our watch,
Ship to shore and go-between.

In a tack's heady
Moment do they steady
Us as we go about,
Voices of the past
Shadows that forecast
to underwrite a word spelt out

In waves of high frequency?
O muse of the ordinary,
Medium and alter ego,
Reverberate in names
Our salvage claims
Lima, Oscar, Victor, Echo.

2

Foot, head, tack,
clew, luff and leech –
Bob McCune seadog
names me parts of a sail.
I thought of Japanese *sensei*
'a life before', 'a teacher'

and stowing the sail
each term sung in me,
a gleam and engine of sound
precise and weatherworn
as meticulously back and forth
we folded into the cloth

sailors of Mesopotamia,
Egyptian mariners,
boatmen of the Middle Sea,
Barbary coastal pirates
or nosing the Indian Ocean
Arabians on their dhow.

Moves of hands that listen
to so many lives before,
long benevolence of the gone
as down in their debt we tap;
leaf-trace and rootstock;
tutoring guests and ghosts.

3

Under the swung boom
Unordinary delirium
Of Joshua Slocum

As out of a morning east
Sudden glimpses of coast.
My father's ghost

2

Paradox of a steady passion,
Trappist lover's feast and ration;

Clearheaded joy, sober kick,
Trembling music's arithmetic;

A clove hitch that holds when taut,
Perfect rhymes that shape a thought,

Flow and sand of filter bed,
Tip and tig of heart and head;

Wings lift-off, a braking fin,
Words run wild my pulse reins in.

3

Another dawn watch begun at ten to seven
As light breaks into the wind's anarchy;
A steady head but no haven heaven,
Hopkins forever out in the swing of the sea.
To know the ropes, always to think ahead,
Again same shipshape rule and routine;
Everything coiled, made off, cleated,
Sails flaked or stowed, a readied unforeseen.
Over and over a day's lone discipline
As my white horses whelm and overcome,
Waters brimmed and harrowed in a wind's fetch,
Crests ridden, the troughs weathered within,
The green swell seldom in the haven's dumb;
In every squall a heart's range and stretch.

House

1 *Storeys*

Hub and core
Of our daily round
A bottom floor;
Kitchen, lounge, porch
Suit us down to the ground.

But sorting realities of day
Climb one flight
To shadow play
In sleep and dream
Second storied night.

Then, win or lose
My attic tenancy.
Floored by the muse,
A hard landing.
Top-flight of fancy.

2 *Corners*

Softly and aside
Forgotten by the vacuum
Forgiven by the broom
In dusty half-lit angles of a room
Our daydreams ride

Their cock-horse
Ring-fingered, fancy-free
To bell-toed Banbury,
Footloose music of reverie
Running its sweet course.

O Wizard of Oz,
Memory's wand,
Tip our too fond
Balance, somehow slip beyond,
Conjure what never was.

Make-believe. Our delirium.
Dreamer and sojourner,
Little Jack Horner
Sit in your delighted corner
Pulling out your plum.

A world in the head.
But deeper, wider,
The muse insider
Unreels from Miss Muffet's spider
An endless silken thread.

3 *Echoes*

An underground desire to bloom
Sows
And grows
The damask rose
Of hopes that now as memory recompose.

Harmonics of abode, geography of echoes
Embrace
A trace
Of daily footpace,
Fall and print on years of staircase.

Our covenants loamed in time and space
Become
The shalom
Of every room
We walk. Mellow somnabulance of home.

4 *Shades*

How still all holders of our house abide
In an ether where secret decibels relay
Things mumbled under breath or cried
At night in a dream's *esprit d'escalier*.
Half-sentences of an interrupted story
Our lives and space seem almost to subsume;
Creaky resonance of each imagined memory
In the infinite daydream of a lived-in room.
How shadows caught in silence overhear
Voices of those who come to take our place
For this late supper *à deux* by candlelight
When swapped news allows a day cohere
In broken bread of evening's face to face.
Across a room our ghosts now smile goodnight.

IOU

1

Two brass pans hung from a scale-beam
On a balance of years –
One with childhood hurt, one with a dream.

Once a cocky young man with somersault
Moods and humours,
Huffs and counter-time, a jibbing colt.

The iconoclast bravado of damaged memory
Shadow boxed
A father's shadow in all the powers that be.

Deeply a body remembers and seems to nestle
Kinks and clinches,
Reflexes of old injuries in sinew and muscle.

Knots and hang-ups. So many demons to redeem
Or hold at bay.
But a boy in me still carried an infinite dream.

Two brass pans hung from a scale-beam.
O love me long enough to counter-weigh.

2

Fumbled bids to thank you
Fall on different ears
According to your moment's ebb or flow.

Sometimes a dismissive overview:
'No matter what with the years
Somehow you'd have had to mellow';

Others nothing (I hope) you rue
Just a sigh that appears
To tot things up: 'I don't know

'How I managed what we went through!'
In swings and mood careers
A relentless singing vertigo.

So again a scribbled IOU.
I sought him in streets and squares...
I held him and would not let him go.

3

Faithful voyager as push comes to shove
There you are again to bail me out,

Thimbling dry an ocean out of love.
Or for years it must have seemed like that

As the restless boat of my nature changed tack
Shifted so suddenly onto a different course,

Me almost overboard, you dragging me back.
Full and by, zigzag beats and detours

Or learning to slacken sheets and bear away,
When to ride it out or go with the flow.

Rack and pinion, the long haul of everyday,
Course made good, years of common cargo,

All that weathers us in what we weather.
Still my mistress mariner. And still together.

Three Minutes

1

It was one of those three-minute machines.
Passport size. The black curtain drawn
Aside, we huddled together for dear life
on a wobbly, twirlable stool and waited
forever trying to hold onto our smile
till the explosive bulb fixed us in its blitz.

It must have stuck in at the back of a drawer.
Anyhow, the other day we dropped on the floor,
your hair loosely pinned up behind
and there I am in a yellow summer shirt,
your arm around me, squeezing into the booth;
yoked and both facing into the light.

2

Riddle me a riddle of how we season.
We change as our world changes;
Conspiracy of time, a growing treason

Of never ever the same twice.
The minute we kiss and touch
A slippage, an elusive paradise.

Hidden in a mind's skittish inscape
Our half-desires and fictions,
We juggle even dreams we shape.

Biographies we delicately rearrange,
Selves we slough off,
Constancy of constant change.

Flesh sapped five years ago,
A hide already shed,
I sweet a body I barely know.

3

Zigzag and detour. All our wafts and drifts.
Broadening in ways we've vaguely understood.

Targets a minute alters as our viewpoint shifts;
Things we do we never thought we would.

Light, shape and size a varying assemblage
Our lens can either narrow or magnify.

Yet somewhere in the brain we hold an image
As if there's more to seeing than meets the eye.

Remember π a stylish dolmen in a row
Of easy figures? The terms 'constant', 'variable?'

Diameter and circumference a constant ratio.
In any circle however big or small.

Our growth ring widens it's looping parallel.
Breadth and compass. Love's proportioned circle.

Weathering

1

Winds back and freshen
As mare's tails, wispy and thin,
Puff and huddle and darken.
Although the signs were ominous –
A depression moving steadily in –
How easily a gale creeps up on us!

Too fretful about a squall
To see the moment, too deep in detail
To notice the overall
As clouds had gathered and huffed.
You could teach the devil himself to sail
If only he could look aloft.

All seemed plain sailing.
Then, suddenly, as though from nowhere
A moody gust. Yet seeing
How I'm just as thin-skinned,
Why didn't I sense the cooler air,
Prepare to slacken and spill the wind?

2

Mostly a tiff that seemed about nothing
Or anyhow something that had nothing to do
With what we'd begun to argue about,
Although from the start I knew
I'd have to winkle out
A hurt you'd been for weeks mutely nursing.

I think we'd fall into a pattern.
It's you who'd held our lives steady,
So how could I ride out a billow
Of sudden humours? Already
My psyche hits Skid Row
As we seesaw and gainsay out of turn.

A heated logic's riddle-me-re.
But I'd fail to find the middle ground
And play Hamlet at the end of his tether
Until you'd come around
To pull us both together,
End up blaming yourself for blaming me.

3

In the eye of a storm still to find perspective,
To slide a lens from zoom to a wider view

And set a moment's detail against our life.
In holding off, my love, I'm holding you.

The years it takes to learn a double vision!
I'm standing back a fraction for your sake

Trying at once to pan and zero in on
How everything and nothing is at stake.

Bifocal ardour. A space to allow me to keep
On trusting even if you seem to stand aloof,

A close-up that still retains its wider sweep
And holds my need for warmth at one remove.

Imperfect metal tempered to a new resilience;
My presence somehow nearer for its distance.

Stains

1

Honeyed in our aftermath we lie
Hand in hand to stare at where
A drink I spilt above had left
It's watermark tracing out
Across our boudoir ceiling exotic
Archipelagos of browning lands,
Mini-continents with sandy shores
Thrown up on a plaster fault line
That seems to map a travelled world
Voyages charted in oceans of white.

I drift in and out of sleep
Content in a hazy borderland
Between the real and understood
An interregnum in the mind when
Our time together begins to flicker
And gather in one moment before
It again disperses around a sepia
Atlas of half-memories that shift
And float along a landmass shelf
Dreaming onwards side by side.

So many regions unexplored,
Exotic islands of pleasure foregone,
Realms left forever unseen,
Atlantis of the might have been
Or even an ordinary country passed
By, some *terra firma* where
We might have settled but knew
We had to keep a course and steer
Our ship by each other's star
Or be a lotus-eater left behind.

2

The ways things would spill and fall,
Blotches and seepage of how it is,
Chances of lives that overlap.

With someone else who knows who
We'd have become: another map,
Unlike patterns, a different stain.

If I hadn't let myself be chosen
Who do you think would have lain
Here now catnapping in your bed?

I puzzle over what never was
Gazing at the watermarks overhead.
Your mission to bring an outsider in.

Anchor of loners, tender of wounded.
I wonder who else you might have been,
Of all your odd men out which

You'd have wifed? The sergeant dreamer,
The gambler who'd later strike it rich?
Good night then Madam Millionaire!

3

Each choice has left another choice behind
Among all the *we*'s we might have been.

At every turn our design redefined.
Indelible ink of being. Our stains are in.

A living batik of knotted dips and prints
Where gain is also loss and every tie,

Anything chosen at once loosens and tightens,
A steeped folding soaking in its dye.

Whatever now our map, our seeped traces,
The stains of other selves are long outdated,

Our story absorbed into the other's face's
Lines and creases, both of us implicated

In all the twists and hues impressed so far.
Tell me your love. I'll tell you who you are.

Tandem

1

Perhaps just one of my so many vagaries,
A whirlwind idea I'd talked you into
And off we pushed uphill against the breeze

Riding hell for leather our sheeny new
Black heavy metal roadsters. I think
We both pedalled a phantom bicycle for two,

Each of us secretly striving to keep in sync
With the other's alternating second wind.
Down in Kilkenny there's marble black as ink.

Afraid to let one another down we'd grinned
And borne our knee-jerk reaction to the strain –
We should have said, even been more disciplined.

But to choose the foothill of a Wicklow mountain
The long way around, such sweated circuities
When we could have travelled a duller Kildare plain?

Our manic headlong pedal-driven intensities.
One hand steers, the other urging our knees,
We climb the greasy dream of marble cities.

2

So few days before we'd got together.
Headfirst we struck out
Hot in our leather
Learning as we went
A mutual comether.

And only weeks before we'd both sign on
For wherever it would lead,
Fragile liaison
Of whispers and covenants,
Our tender marathon.

Even from the start I'm sure you'd found
The going tough. An obstinate streak
The contrary high ground,
Slews and swings,
The long way around.

If only I'd understood the highway code
But we rode against the wind;
We might have toed
The line, instead we went
The mountain road.

A rough ride far over and above
Anything you'd reckoned on;
Push come to shove,
Holding a delicate balance
Ad-libbingly you love.

3

Down in Kilkenny it is reported...
Our boneshakers parked in a yard below
We're fetched up on a lodging house bed
Hearts pumping and drumming *fortissimo*,

Too exhausted to even think of making hay
I've wandered off into an infant sleep
Begun again to breathe the flush and sway
Of wind as poised we tackle another steep

Mountain road apace and I wonder whether
Bodies have a will of their own or if we relax
Into a double rhythm pedalling together,
Each of us picking up where the other slacks.

A trade balance subtler than *quid pro quo*,
Intricate lovemaking of motion in tandem.
I yield control and let the steering go.
Please don't wake me out of this dream.

No-man's-land

1

Still my boyhood's Aran trance.
At bedtime when I lit a sconce
Already I'd begun a long fall,
An actor who came to be his role.
Perhaps to understand is to become
Whatever it is we yearn to fathom.

No distance. At any rate not for me
The chill removes of anthropology
Or pieced shards of a scholar's vase.
I can only say whatever it was
I'd known I had to learn by love.
From inside out. Hand in glove.

O woken Belshazzar of Babylon
Over against the candlestick and on
A whitewashed wall a hand has written:
Be glad you weren't so hard-bitten
Or so old so young to notice where
A shadow's fingers wrote despair.

To drink Belshazzar's empty cup?
So hard to say the game is up,
My heritage on me a speckled bird.
Though I can no longer risk my word,
A hopeless hoping swings between
What is and still what might have been.

2

Before we'd met you'd long decoded
The scribble on the whitewashed wall
It would take me years to read.

Did a young man's fever renew
Your yielded hopes or was it
All that's big and lavish in you

Going with the flow of how I was,
Eternal woman falling again
For a driven male, a man with a cause?

The same abundance that understood
When sobered Belshazzar had seen
The ghostwritten scrawl and could

No longer jeopardise his muse.
Once watching as you lit a candle
I ask why you came to choose

To love me. Laughing you tell me
How much it weighted that I had been
A citizen of your childhood country.

3
And yes, yes, things will fade, things change.
A millennium or two tiny in a bigger scheme.

The star gazing grave builders of Newgrange,
Movers and shakers all dwindle in a daydream.

Did they too once read the shadow's scrawl,
Know the strange forlornness of no-man's-land?

Even when we decipher the letters on the wall
I suppose we changelings never understand.

To love what is and not what might have been
I serve my craft. But yet we keep our word.

Year by year I've lived my boyhood trance.
A sonority, turns and vibes of phrase, my live-in

Lover's unbroken code of bed and board.
What lonely ghosts sleep-walk our dalliance.

Ceremony

1

I want to remember Friday evenings
We dressed up just to go nowhere
and carefully laid a table for us both,
pretended we were each other's guest
and host as we lit a scented candle,
wooers tending the smallest need
we talked as though we rarely met
allowing ceremony undo the hex
of everydayness, of half-said things,
what we should have heard but missed
as if round and routine both bind
and cast a spell we need to break.
We date, we dally, paying court
to broach the sabbath of ourselves.

2

Slow repetition of sober days,
An actor's lines over and over
Till every twitch of the tongue obeys.

Sluggish mornings a struggle to cope.
Tumbling, tumbling acrobat
Behind the smiling dancer on the rope.

Scaled hours against the flow
A pianist's years of finger drills
Before the encore and the low bow.

Hell, high-water. Thick and thin.
Gain and build-up of steady pace,
A refusal to give up or in.

Slack *accelerando* of covenant,
Strange freedoms of discipline
Pirouette in the glory of an instant.

Acupoint of joy. Harnessed catharsis.
Everything new and possible again
An old actor's glow. All for this.

3
Bird flight at sundown.
Afterwards the aftershine.
Infinite moment.

Selves

1

Right from curtain-up a jangle of rapport.
Though maybe even in our first delirium,

Waiting in the wings, selves we'd fallen for
Trusted the shuffle of what we'd yet become.

Improvisation, a plot still in the making.
Utterly involved and still detached enough

To love; double-eyed actors always taking
Our cue from the other maybe we'd pull it off?

Long steady dialogue of gain and surrender,
Theatre in the round, coarse grain of living

Where both can be a borrower and a lender,
Ourselves as much in taking as in giving.

Mix of endless mongrel *you*'s and *me*'s.
Cast and ragbag of our hybrid psyches.

2

Who's this woman I know I've never known?
After thirty years surely through and through

But now out of nowhere a fresh come-on,
Awe and tease of some other stranger you

Who probably didn't exist those years ago
But more than likely ripened as you grew

To play this leading lady I desire to know.
Enter then this queen of hearts on cue

To say if you still recognise the figure I cut?
Prince Hamlet lulled by his tragic flaw

Who somewhere along the line lost the plot
Or a consort whose dream you dreamt you saw?

We both usurp the selves we thought we'd be.
Am I the surprise for you that you're for me?

3

Now a lover and now an *éminence grise*,
The quick changes, the moods we display,

Parts we swap or learn to switch with ease
Gamut of a self's *dramatis personae*.

Fever and fright. Each lead and cameo,
Long years through our paces and routines

With me your opposite star and antihero,
Triumph or flop, all the shifting scenes.

Then suddenly to surge and lose control.
My *femme fatale* again I ogle and squire.

Forever new our throwaway lines of play
As we slip in ripe delight from role to role

To strut our hidden stage of old desire.
Love my glory. Love my feet of clay.

Darkroom

All recreation alone
Off a landing halfway up
A dormitory stairs
Our hightech co-op,
Red-light chamber of pleasures,
Twilight zone.

Patrick McGlade S.J.'s
Photography club,
Den of potassium odours,
Brown bottled lab
Of fixers, enlarger, rollers,
Tin plates to glaze

A slow foggy image
That under my forceps
Begins at last to unblur
As something develops
In a dish I seem to stir
Until you emerge

Some two score years
Off in a haze
Of all that's yet to shape
Logics of fuzz,
Chaos dreams that leap
Their grey frontiers

To redefine a story
While we wait
In the darkroom of a moment
Shade and light
For some future determined
To become a memory

That may have been a dream
On which we focused,
A single rapid exposure
We have to trust
But never can be sure,
A sort of dim

But deeper recollection,
Vague and filtered
We bit by bit adapt
And funnel inward,
A dusky shot snapped
On a lens of perfection

Now fixing in a murk
Of stock solution
Gradual matters of fact
On a bromide silver emulsion,
A Rembrandt effect
Ripening in the dark.

Parkinson's

1

Stealthily. One day that quiver in your ring
Finger. Or my impatience at your squiggling

Such illegible notes. Just your astonishment
Noticing the absence of an old lineament.

Once speedy genes, high-geared and fleet;
At twelve the school's swiftest athlete.

The oils of movement slower to lubricate.
Stiffness, a tremor, that off-balance gait.

A specialist confirms Parkinson's disease.
Failing dopamine. The brain's vagaries.

Then moments of denial. Again so strong
And confident: Those doctors got it wrong.

Your fright is pleading with me to agree.
I bat for time: Maybe, we'll have to see.

What can I do? These arms enfold you.
No matter what, I have and hold you.

And so you must travel painful spendthrift
Windings of acceptance. Giving turns gift.

Together. But is there a closer closeness?
Yet another shift in love's long process.

2

Flustered now by stress,
A need for time,
Days planned, a gentler pace;
Any breeze shivers in your limbs,
My aspen mistress.

Hardy, deep-rooted, light-loving
You learn to endure.
Pioneer tree in fallow or clearing.
A random sigh flutters in your leaves:
O God, I'm tired of shaking

3

Often I wake early to taps on my pillow.
Last evening's tablet at the end of its tether
Your forefinger begins its morning *tremolo*
As if counting in sleep hours lain together.
I think at first you'd pitied an over eagerness,
My jittery hand that spilled half your coffee;
A headstrong giant-killer wobbly and nervous
That slowly over time you'd steadied in me.
Blurs and transfers between fellow travellers.
I couldn't but see your half flirtatious sidelong
Glance at me that both asks and reassures:
Even if I shake I think my spirit is young?
Our years side by side tongued and grooved.
A face is beautiful once a face is loved.

Driving

Often a shade quicker to react
You alert your duller half.
Yet another misfortune staved off.

But sometimes not. I'm all thrown
By a flash countermand
To what I've already reckoned on.

What I ask you do you take me for?
Ah, you wonder how to tell.
And then just supposing I hadn't?

Damned if you do, damned if you don't.
Cleft stick of devotion.
This note on a windscreen to say I'm grateful.

Mistress

Even at the door I hear your school voice,
And am awkward as I slip into your sanctum

A timid copy-bearer approaching with a sum
You'll tot and tick off, doling out your praise.

I sneak a voyeur's glance before you know
I'm standing there at sides of you I rarely see,

Heisenberg cheating a principle of uncertainty
I'm peeping now at this mistress *ex officio*.

Steady performer, gently in charge of it all
'Up you come to the table and show me your sum!'

But I've been spotted. A rumour across a room:
Look teacher! Teacher, look it's Micheal!

Flagrante delicto I glimpse your metamorphosis.
A flash smile turns to reassure my gaucheness.

FULL AND BY

In sailing 'full and by' the aim is to make the best possible progress to windward, the best balance between high pointing and fast footing.

Boatwords (Denny Desoutter)

Savoir donner cette sérénité au bateau, voilà tout l'art du bon marin...ce n'est que de proche en proche que l'on améliore la marche du bateau...

The art of great sailors is no more, and no less than this: to bring harmony to their vessels...you approach perfection through a series of approximations...

JEAN-LOUIS GOLDSCHMID
translated by Peter Davison

Gaze

Ordinary out of the ordinary
Moments
I eye again
Lineaments
That now contain
Traces of a fumbled history,
Love *a fortiori*
Scribbling in faces
Each other's story

And remembered infatuated
Glances,
First eyeings up,
Dalliances
Loop the loop
Of all the years we're mated
And derring-do
Drop in free-fall
As I fell for you.

But a deeper wonder.
Greedy
I craved your all,
Needy,
Any withdrawal
Or doubt and I'd flounder,
Hamlet who'd brood,
And chafe or pout
A blackmail mood.

Some old damage inbred,
Decades spent
Determined to bless
A temperament,
An all-or-nothingness
So long wing-wounded
Or confused or both
At once. Slow
Blundered growth

With so many hurts unshown
Or unshared
Grieves lonely
Unrepaired,
If and *only*
Of how we might have flown
A different way
Forgive us now
Such feet of clay.

Yet what soars between us!
You and me
Flickering delight
In infinity,
Daily flight
In the sun. Madcap Icarus
Whatever I do
Whatever I've done
I home in you

Who has endlessly believed
In what we might
Or what we still
Become. Inflight
Invisible
Repair. Once a thieved
Sly, sideways
Lover's stare.
Now this gaze.

Caprice

1

Vibes that want to jar or risk the duo,
Passing notes too harsh, out of sync,

Mismatched phrasings, uneven tempo,
Clashes as melody hovers on the brink.

O the ease of steady lines! One to one.
Unnerved at every interrupted cadence

It took me years to trust to resolution.
Richness of each mended dissonance.

Caprice and ruses of wild love-making,
Flirted anticipations, playful tension,

Rising sounds retarded enough to hone
An urge, keep accelerating and braking

Pleasure. A quaver held in suspension.
Offbeat discords prime a sweeter tone.

2

Delicious liberty of notes to rove
Extempore
Con amore
As in between the lines we wove
Inaudible noise
Of a middle voice
Underwrites our undersong,
Cantus firmus
Holding us
In melodic progression, headstrong
Silent tenor,
Our rapport.

3

A trace in us, an echo of some tonality,
Whatever loves us before we ever loved,

What loneness ours even as we roved
Out, still signs its key in you and me.

Three decades everything shared and joint.
Flesh of my flesh, bone alongside bone;

More and more together and still alone,
Lines ripening in unison and counterpoint

We hold a pitch and measure as best we can.
The more our rock and rhythm correspond

The longer we long, the further on beyond,
Desire homing towards where desire began

As though from its beginning a tune returns;
Glory of our music how our music yearns.

Duration

1

Open stage, no hiding wings,
Mood swings, every scenario,
Dreams, hurts, coups, failings,
Space to let each other grow,
Our repertoire of knockabout,
Kitchen sink and passion play,
To know our parts inside out,
To choose rehearsed naïveté
Of moments taken one by one.
Often mothered in my wound,
Sometimes do I daughter you?
Subtle timings, shifts of cue,
Day by day played in the round,
Ad-lib an ease of layered duration.

2

Cost analysis of gaffes and failures
As we number over older blunders
Balancing out and taking stock.

Designs, things hearts set on,
Blighted causes, a false dawn,
But how even hindsight wonders,

How we so often got it wrong?
Sometimes you'd known all along,
Both loving and doubting you yielded.

Recalled cringe of once phases,
Youth's labyrinth and vast mazes
And no short-cuts across time's arc.

Let-downs, what didn't go to plan,
Gnaws and rubbing, even chagrin
Tie the slow ravellings of duration.

Again the ultimate sophistication:
To say like Ibsen's Terje Vigen
Best all happened the way it did.

Strange discipline of false scents,
Mistakes we count on now as portents.
Remembered shinings, forgotten dark.

3

But is now an error in some future date?
Pace again battlements Hamlet O'Siadhail

Or say *confusion is not an ignoble state*
(Imperfectly I rhyme with Brian Friel).

Chameleon days, divine dissatisfaction,
Changing scenes, lines I know I forgot,

The constant edits, rewrites or redirection
And yet to believe we haven't lost the plot

But keep on relearning and switching role
As if to follow a plot but not the plotting

As if forgivingly we go improvising on
A performance art still beyond control,

Duration's every knotting and unknotting
Gentling us towards whatever dénouement.

Hostess

In friendships I made the pace
Interfacing
Sometimes for us both; your way instead
A discerning, stable

Concentration of insight,
Jeweller's loupe,
A magnifying glass picking out
Minutiae of care.

Whatever my need to share,
Little doubt
In other friends the prism I hold up
Refracts your light,

Hostess queen of table,
Wide-hearted
Tenderer to guest or stranger, embracing
All I embrace.

At Sea

Jets whine overhead.
Who will be lonely for whom?
One silver gull cries.

Yoked we throw our light.
That one will be first to go.
A twin star untwinned.

Question

On our shed's south wall it's spring.
Clianthus puniceus has opened out
clusters of crimson parrots' bills,
drooped bunches of lobsters' claws.
In a neighbour's garden cotoneaster
fires with berries a chill sunlight.
Our two silver birches have shot
their buds to fuzz a colder outline,
in their limbs a Swedish refrain:
Det är ju godt att vi är två
It's so good that we are two.

These lines now since student days
a minor keyed harvest folksong
vad jag fäller, du raker in –
what I cut down, you rake in
And now three dozen years beyond
as we play out our third score
it's pining tune haunts the more,
winds down darker in our time
an austere three-time rhythm
Det är så tråkigt att ensamt gå –
So backbreaking to walk alone.

Would this be the hardest season?
Unshared days between our birches'
burgeon and when the soft lime
mouse ears so noiselessly unfold
And early March wind sways
a tandem leaning as their branch tips
almost touch. In the falling tones
of a melody again the low warm
swish of a scythe. *Bak i skuggan*
Går en ängel och räfser in –
In the shadow an angel gathers in.

If

Maybe
Together. If one must go
First? In imagined schism
Our tentative enquiry:
If you were

Alone
Would you fall again in love?
A slow chiselling realism
In your reply: enough
To shape one stone.

But me...
I don't know how to know.
Trusting hues of your prism,
If I was so lucky,
I think I'd dare.

Passage

So our boat ploughs on,
The bows still scudding with ease,
Old homing salmon.

Off course. No pinching.
A sail full and by the breeze.
One butterfly wing.

The tune yearning plays,
A song humming in the wire,
Wind sung in our stays.

Voyage we still dream.
Long perspective of desire.
Port's fugitive gleam.

Against

Every qualm or doubt
Thrashed out,
Talked over,
Non-stop Hamlet,
Sleep-tosser, night-walker,
Set

Against a fern's silence,
Calmly intense,
Contemplative,
A frond-still
Kind of live and let-live,
Gentle

Unfolding in good time;
Steady sap-climb,
Leaf-stir
And shining through.
Shalom-finder. Heart-ponderer.
You.

Day

Our days were forever.
Forever now one more day
New under the sun.

Double-blossomed lives.
Full and by. Then, to die well.
Gently petals fall.

Our love spooling out
Sun-up-ness and sun-down-ness.
Wisdom's crimson thread.

Cameo x 3

1

Warm but matter of fact.
Mover and dreamer. All your inbred
But's and *and*'s.

Rite-breaker and reverer,
Woman of action for all your worth
But visionary,

Both a doer and hearer.
Martha cumbered, down-to-earth.
Attentive Mary.

Twin strands.
Funambulist on a crimson thread.
Love's balancing act.

2

Daily affirmer.
Years at school conducting a class,
Whispers, laughter, murmur;
Your ruler a baton's hoisted upbeat.

Grown-ups you meet
By chance, sudden glances of delight
At seeing you in the street.
Recall a half-forgotten bond.

First face beyond
The home and cradle. Halfway house.
Life's brokeress. A fond
Voice calling towards the world.

3

In a mirror you hung on the wardrobe
Through our open bedroom door
A lampshade's white paper globe
Moons before
First light floods our gable-window.

I reflect how I'd thought years ago
You'd paint and already dreamt up
Some Van Gogh blue and yellow,
Large buttercup
Suns burning an Arles noon.

Instead a calmer composition of moon
Framed by banister against a crimson
Window-pane. *Clair de lune*
At Booterstown.
Our life together your still-life.

Crimson Thread

My love, my love along the slopes of Gilead,
This is our Eden before the bitter apricot.
How unimaginable now our story if we had
Never met, never shaped each other's plot.
Fracture and hurt of a once bruised youth,
Sores healed by wine and oil and spice.
Kiss of life. Shulammite's mouth-to-mouth.
My wounds bound up in second paradise.
Over and over. Season by season by season,
I'm older than my mother's crimson moment.
Our slow grown plot of risks and pardon
As father cries how things would be different,
If things were again. O heart's secret treason!
My sister, my bride...I come to your garden.

Again from under
Scarlet cords of winter fruit
A sumac burgeons.

We roved out all in our youth and prime.
Both real and unreal it seems somehow
Like reading a novel for the second time
To recall our unfolding in the light of now.
So much that fell almost as if by accident,
Twists and corners we couldn't see or gauge,
The plot gradually entangled as we went
That will have been our story page by page.
Two so close. Two so utterly different.
Clash and blur become a rich repair,
Secrets held to love more open-eyed,
Lives sweet against a crimson moment.
Chalk or cheese of what we are or share.
Lived-in paradox of decades side by side.

Deep deeper yellow
Prepares a crimson moment.
A sumac's leaf falls

Dew, spice, honey, wine and milk,
Bone of my bone, flesh of my flesh
Wear again for me the damson silk
I take as given and still begin afresh.
Awake o north wind, come south wind....
Never enough just to have rubbed along.
Promise of promises nothing can rescind.
All or nothing. All is Solomon's Song.
I come to my garden, my sister, my bride.
Eat friend, drink and be drunk with love
And every moment I think I'm satisfied
Wakes me to desires I'm dreaming of.
In Solomon's blue curtain a cord of covenant,
A crimson thread until the crimson moment.